Do the longings of migration and displacement have a musicality? The verses in *Las Piedrecitas* are acts of close listening—across language, across space, across time, across embodiment. To read them is to share in that listening, itself a practice that the collection's many speakers learn to do in struggle and in jubilance. The music here resounds because it refuses to dwell at the pitch of trauma, the tone of crisis that so often gets carelessly attached to brownness. Cerna attends carefully to *las piedrecitas*, the very pebbles of experience that are not always hard or coarse but sometimes "soft enough…to just exist." These ambivalences are dignified rather than disavowed, silence and rest as poignant as the noise of living. That living, Cerna sings, can be thriving.

—Travis Chi Wing Lau, author of the *The Bone Setter*, *Paring*, and *Vagaries*

www.blacklawrence.com

Executive Editor: Diane Goettel
Cover Design: Zoe Norvell
Cover Art: "Tending Wounds" by Octavio Quintanilla
Book Design: Amy Freels

In June of 2023, Black Lawrence Press welcomed numerous existing and forthcoming Nomadic Press titles to our catalogue. The book that you hold in your hands is one of the forthcoming Nomadic Press titles that we acquired.

Published 2024 by Black Lawrence Press.
Printed in the United States.

Las Piedrecitas

Noelia Cerna

For my father, for inspiring this collection and loving me through every stage of our relationship.

For my mother, for showing me the true meaning of strength, wisdom, and beauty.

For my daughter, for giving me joy every single moment and for making me the softest version of myself.

For me, for surviving unspeakable things in order to write these poems and being brave enough to believe in this collection.

And for every brown girl that is still becoming. May you become bravely and allow yourselves to do so gently.

Contents

"*On the long-roofed steamship piers one is in a country that is no longer here and not yet there.*"

—F. Scott Fitzgerald, *Tender Is the Night*

***

"*I don't like parties because I don't like talking in circles. I get too nervous, worry someone will ask me about where I'm from, and I won't know.*"

—Giovanna Lomanto, *I Am Your Immigrant Daughter*

Containing Multitudes

Professor Wayne Zade

Creative Writing became a cottage industry in American academic life a half century ago, at first on the college and university levels and then also on the secondary and elementary school levels. Culturally, this was, and is, a good thing. Students learn about literature, its powers and saving graces, "from the inside out." In an electronic age in which literacy levels have tended to plunge, students writing poems and stories can confront challenges and obstacles in their lives and in lives around them in constructive ways. Even if students pass through these classes because they seem easy, and most do only that, they benefit. Other students stick with writing and grow into new and more profound challenges. *Las Piedrecitas* began as Noelia Cerna's senior thesis in English, and I directed her in the project. Reading the book as a fully-developed collection of poems, developed over the course of some 13 years, is to witness her perseverance, pride, and power.

The news contains countless stories about the politics of immigration. Migrants fleeing intolerably oppressive and dangerous conditions for a chance at a better life for themselves and their families in America, as people have always done, have become pawns in political chess games dominated by ruthless leaders trying to appeal to voters' worst instincts. The family in this book of poems—father, mother, daughter, sister—fled Nicaragua in the 1990s and settled in Arkansas. The poems chart the daughter's childhood, adolescence and early adulthood, and womanhood, and the many challenges, defeats, and small victories she has lived. In other words, "the news" becomes deeply personal in these poems.

The costs of resettlement are heavy and high: "But like all dreams there comes a time to wake" ("DACA"). We see the father go from playful, funny, and musical, to sad, worried, overprotective, and controlling, not only of family traditions and customs (and language), but also of his daughters: "You never expected to become the thing you hate so much." The daughter who speaks the poems will one day come to say, "I have fought against your hostile takeover / for thirty years" ("Dictators").

School, education, for this woman presents the difficulties of assimilation, the trading in and out of Spanish and English, and the challenges of finding oneself, educating oneself: "Double major! It is perfectly rational to study both poetry and biology. Own your intelligence / and tell your advisor to shove it because the only one that knows what you're capable of accomplishing is you!" ("Advice (to My College Self)")

Social life, dating, coming to terms with one's sexuality, are perilous and pernicious in college for this woman, and yet they are experience hard won. "That frat boy will rape you and it will be OK because seven years later you'll be able to tell the desperate girl on the crisis text line whose boyfriend just raped her that this is not the end. / Trust me. I have survived to make poetry." ("Advice (to My College Self)")

Survival for the woman who speaks—sings, in perhaps an ironic nod to the father of her childhood—the poems in this book live in relationships with several important women: Maria, an immigrant Hispanic woman who is a janitor at Walmart Corporate, where the speaker works in an office job; Karen, a kind of mother-surrogate, friend, and confidante, who dies; and finally, most importantly, the speaker's mother, Alna, whose poem is presented in call-and-response form with one of her own ("A Kyrie for Dreams").

Perhaps the book's culmination and fulfillment come in "Dear Timid Latina Girl," a love letter to the speaker herself, "in full goddess form." After so many doubts, insecurities, violations, and setbacks, the speaker arrives at the quiet celebrations of forgiveness and acceptance of self: "Until you are ready to step boldly into the world as everything you are, these quiet / celebrations are enough. You are enough, brown girl…you always have been." One way to read *Las*

Piedrecitas is as a kind of "Song of Myself," not only a celebration of self but also of all a self contains, "multitudes," as in Whitman's case, citizens of more than one country, fellow travelers of the world and life. And there are echoes in the book of Whitman's long lines, which are sometimes regarded as operatic, and I like to imagine Noelia delivering some of the poems in performance formats, which she does often, confidently, and successfully.

There is news in this book, good and bad news. But the book reminds me, in Pound's words, that "Poetry is news that stays news."

Las Piedrecitas

He'd stand guard over me making sure the tourists didn't get too close
keeping an eye on the older, local boys and the men as I ran
through the grass

Our park was in Nicaragua
Las Piedrecitas was Papi's and Tutu's
"Tutu" his name for me
"Piedritas" my name for it
I could never say it right but it remained "our" park even so
He would take me to play there as often as he could

At my favorite fountain he would hold my hand as I climbed
on to the edge, circled it pretending to fall
so that daddy could catch me
He would sometimes run with me
picking me up high off the ground
not having to set his gaze on those around me
so long as he had me in his arms
shouting and laughing
until he put me down once more
and went back to his careful watch

I would run from statue to statue the gray stone cool beneath my
hands
He would watch me climb and mimic the statue's pose
smiling at him and waving
He would watch me climb, the statues guarding me
from the natives and tourists
who might lure me away

with promises of candy
should he become distracted
by the conversations
taking place around us
while the statues
set their steady stone gazes
towards the edges of the park
and beyond
towards a future
and a place
he could not see
beyond Nicaragua's borders

Tortuguita

The fruit sat
in my plastic
Rainbow Brite
bowl
untouched 'cause I was
picky
"Tortuguita!"
my grandpa says
"Termina tu cena"
"No me gusta!"
I whine
pushing the soggy
pineapple
around
"Como se dice en Ingles?"
my mom asks
and I think
and say
"I no like, um, la piña!"
pleased
I smile
"Quiero jugar!"
I laugh
So daddy
picks me up
takes me
to the beach
and I listen
to the waves

and smell the salt
on the wind
sweaty
playing
'til the sun goes down
Then gallo pinto
and chayote for dinner
left untouched
then bed
where I
fall asleep
and listen to the waves

Cantos y Playas

He would sing
with his guitar
My sister sang with him

He would sing
to mom, and me,
my sister sang along
We'd go to the beach
to swim
and drink pitaya
and
Fanta
when it got too hot
"Papi! Los caballos, mira!"
I would squeal
and he would rent one
and we'd ride
across the sand
Shaking with laughter
I'd turn to him
and say
"Eres mas lindo
que un perfumen!"
And he would smile,
pick up his guitar
and play
songs my mom
knew in English

and he would
harmonize with her
and she'd teach us
and my sister
laughed with me
to hear
such funny words
but we'd sing them
anyways

And he would sing
to me
so I would not feel
left out

and the ocean
sang along
a rolling
steady beat
Mi familia,
mi hogar
the smell of salt
was happiness;
felicidad
and home

Pajarito

Mami loves birds   We listen to them sing
and she smiles as they fly by   Sometimes

the birds are hurt   She picks them up and
teaches me how to help   Some we save

Some we lose   Mami sings them songs and talks
to them   and the pajaritos listen   y yo sonrío

cuando cantan   Today we lose one   and Mami
picks out a butter dish   places him gently

inside   He is buried outside   Mami says
there will be other birds that need our songs

Pajaritos   y   cantos   always find each other
so we play outside   as the birds

fly

              fly

                             above

Tourism and Soda

The tourists
could never figure it out
"La bolsita se corta asi"
my father would explain to them
"Cut the corner of the bag, like this."
They would tilt the bag
awkwardly
and hold it close
to their bodies
spilling the liquid
down their overly expensive tops

The vendors on the sidewalks
lined with palm trees
would sell soda in bags
from their brightly painted carts
to the passersby
And yet,
they could never understand
how to drink it

"Van a botar la soda!"
one vendor would say
scratching his head
in amazement
and amusement

My friends and I
would show the tourists
how to tip the soda
to the back of the bag
so that they could cut the corners
and drink from them

"Why can't you people just
sell them in cups?
Like normal folks?"
one woman asked

We would simply laugh
and respond
"Pura vida"
as we watched the soda
dribble down their shirts
and mingle with the dirt
beneath their feet

Dirt that was not good enough
to soil their Nikes

America

The day came
when we had to go
to a place
that seemed so far away
Our house was sold
all our toys too
except my Odie dog
I held him
and my daddy's hand
as we walked
up to the plane
"No me quiero ir"
I cried
clinging to Odie's
soggy ears
"Tutu, estas conmigo amor"
my dad said
hugging me
and quietly humming Nino Bravo

I sat between him
and my mom
"Look—that is our new home"
my mom said
"Home?"
"Amor—nuevo hogar"
Clinging to my daddy's hand
I stepped
onto the Arkansas soil

Odie tightly held
my daddy too
"Hello!
How are you?"
a man said
I stared
and gripped
my daddy's hand
The man smiled at me
and walked away
as my daddy

led us out
humming once more
I practiced
"Hello, how are you?"

When Dancing with the Sandinistas

The red and black flag
waved slowly in the breeze
its four white letters
shining in the sun
My father's sad eyes
watched its every move
with an angry bitterness
I'd never seen before
"Tan linda mi Nicaragua"
he'd said absently,
quietly,
mumbling under his breath
cursing the Sandinistas

He spoke of the Nicaragua before—
before the ugly flags
and ruined plazas
before the bits of road
were pulled up
to make trenches
in case of gunfire
before the overwhelming weight
each wrinkled face carried
as it passed us
in the heat—
His Nicaragua
where ignorant tourists
wouldn't spout
their perceptions

and ideologies
about a government system
that they could never fully understand

He remained quiet
from then on
but I could see the pain
welling behind his gaze
of an injustice suffered
that could never
be made right again

And it was "his" land
we both knew
that could never be
passed down to me

DACA

The definition of a dream is a person or thing perceived to be perfect.

We call them Dreamers
the thing perceived to be perfect is a place
a land whispered about behind lace curtains
a land spoken of like paradise
beneath swaying palm trees

Mothers in brightly colored shirts dress their daughters
in ankle-length skirts
and as they comb their hair into braids
whisper in their ears
"Soon you'll be in a place where you are seen
as more than a future mother or cook
One day soon mija you will be somewhere
your mind is valued
where you will be worth more than the children
or entertainment you have to offer

Fathers supervising their sons as they guide the plows
tell them soon they will see a place where their value
won't be placed on how calloused
their hands have become
that they will soon send them to a land
where they can be doctors and earn a living with their minds
instead of their spines
where they won't have to raise livestock
simply because that's what their fathers did
only if they choose to

Fathers with dark skin weathered by the unforgiving sun
begin to believe that they will see their daughters grow
before the violence of the drug cartels
steals quinceañeras and weddings from them
Mothers wrinkled and tired with years of child rearing
and hours spent in rivers washing clothes by hand
cooking over hot stoves in unyielding heat
imagine a land flowing with more than a small ration
of arroz y frijoles
where ribs aren't so easily seen
and children sleep with full bellies
where little hands can hold a pen
instead of a shovel
or an instrument
instead of a crop
where hopes are not foolish
and futures include more than a plow
and a day spent breaking the unforgiving soil

But like all dreams there comes a time to wake
The alarm will ring and every child with braided hair
and hand-me-down clothes will lay down their books
put away their instruments and find a way
to fit their soft hands around shovels
and plows
hot stoves
and babies born far too early

They will learn how to form calluses around tools as unforgiving as
their futures.

Moving Away

The moving van arrives
as the sounds
of the Spanish guitar
drift from my father's bedroom

The cultural expectation
of remaining at home
until married
drifts away
amidst the crunch
of the U-Haul's tires

He is my culture
imposing and unyielding
I am his dream
broken and lost

My father plays an array
of childhood favorites
as I wrap my culture
gently in tissue paper
and place it neatly beneath
my dreams for tomorrow

Volcano

"Después de mi el diluvio."
"After me the flood."

This experience—no flood,
instead she is
a river—of magma
no collection
of water
but volcano
all beauty from a distance
as the sun parts the rainforest
and her slope rises
before his hungry eyes
her magnificence
framed by the jungle mist
peak kissing the heavens
only distance diminishes her
makes her look like something
that can be conquered
something that can be tamed

Perhaps he'll scale to the top
camp within her crater
spend nights
rejuvenated by her heat
intoxicated by her dormant hum

He remains—unaware
her roots
reach the earth's core
unaware that she can
and will come alive
attuned to a careless touch
to a loveless word
always watching
he mistakes climbing for claiming
misnames her mountain, molehill
instead of lava keeper
the destroyer of worlds

He runs screaming into the jungle
as the first rumbles
of a goddess stirring
shake the foundation beneath
his conquering feet
planter of flags
arrogant namer of things
that have names
older than his history
that have stories
peaking before
his own Genesis

Quivering little boy
shivering boy man
running to hide from the volcano
he thought he could break
into valley
he thought he could charm to sleep

Real beauty—
magnificently held,
fascinating to touch
to lay his lips upon
so deadly
to the wrong hands
so violent
to the unprepared
seeming so slow
for being so ancient
for being asleep too long
but burning the world around him
letting him believe for a moment
he can escape
her holy

Dictators

When the gunshots started
to pop
in the depths of those jungles
you called home
you knew
the beast on your heels
demanded fight
or flight

When the Sandinistas
first started constructing
guerilla trenches
in the roadways
started patrolling the streets
in their tanks
rationing food
and changing currencies
you first decided to fight

You never expected
to become
the thing you hate so much
dictators
aren't restricted
to governments

When you put
your wife
and two young daughters

on that plane bound for the promised land
you swore
that we would never see a foreign flag
forced into our hearts
yet here I am
playing the part of the refugee

I have fought
against your hostile takeover
for thirty years
I have burnt my mind down to ashes
ripped out pieces of my self-confidence
changed the flags hanging
from my self-worth
until I no longer recognized
my own identity

Did you ever notice the flames?
The settling dust
from the demolitions?
Or were you too busy
dividing your love
into weekly rations?
Too busy
writing out your demands?

Dad
I have fought to win your pride so long
that I've forgotten my own dreams

So I choose flight

I may not be fleeing a country
this time

but blood
is a much harder thing
to tear away than soil

Dances and Corners

My father was a boxer trained in Nicaragua.

In the faint light of the rising orange sun, before the fresh bread
vendors begin lining the streets with their rosquillas- and picos-
filled carts and their cosa-de-horno-filled pans lining the sidewalks,
he learned to run mile after mile after mile past the colorful lines of
cement-walled houses, their pink, yellow, and orange exteriors
flying past in a blur, 'til the sun-baked clay of the tiled streets
became too unbearable to run on, in the heat of the midday, he
would rehearse the art of the boxer's dance
on the red clay dirt, soil rising from the ground his feet keeping
rhythm with his trainers steady cries as the songs of the bright red,
green, and blue macaws
rang overhead

By the time he stepped into the ring he had trained his bones to take
hit after hit, left hook over right jab, cross and then uppercut.
Learned how to slice open a wound to relieve the pressure of
building blood—that uncomfortable tension of heat and discomfort
bubbling up from beneath already bruising skin, slide Vaseline over
it, and keep going. He taught his mind that "can't" did not exist, that
"tired" was just a word, that pain was mental.
He trained his body completely into his control.
My father was unstoppable, fearless.

It only made sense that one of his children would become like him.
A fighter.
He would stand in our kitchen, tell me to put my hands up and
show me how quickly fists can find kidneys,

placed them in the proper position to protect my chin
and walked me through his favorite series of hooks, jabs and strikes.
Laughing he would throw surprise punches, showed me how
quickly matches can shift
if you're too slow
if you get too comfortable

But my match would take place in a different arena.
He has never understood my opponent, how someone can lose to an
intangible force, to a demon no one else can see. He doesn't realize
that battling depression means accepting there are parts of myself
that will never fully be in my control. He cannot comprehend the
idea that no amount of training can turn me into a machine. Does
not know that so often fighting for my life means to fight this hard
for something I'm not even sure that I want.

But what his scarred hands do know is that feeling of swinging only
to find air. The desperation that builds when a fighter can't land a
hit. That moment you feel the burn of the ropes cutting into your
back.

He knows the signs of a fighter that is ready to quit.
A fighter that is one hit away from a knockout, the familiar limp of
legs too weak to keep their rhythm.
And he refuses to let me quit.
He tells me that in boxing the corner is there to urge you on. To
push you in the hardest moments of a fight,
to tell you to give it one more round.

He takes me by the shoulders, looks me in my eyes and says:
"Baby one more round.
Give me all you've got.
Don't put your hands down.

Don't give up.
Give me one more round."

His voice cracks with desperation and fear. My Nicaraguan father
who has lived through a violent communist takeover and stared
down the barrel of an AK-47 is terrified. He may not understand my
mind but he knows that this is the type of fight that ends lives
and the only way out is through.
Mental illness and depression are foreign to him but he's been a
fighter his whole life

so he slicks up my gloves, oils up my cheeks
to deflect the blows if only momentarily and gives me a firm shove
back into the center of the ring. Tells me to keep my hands up and
to hang on for just one more round.
I don't know if he will ever fully understand this battle but for this
moment he is standing in my corner
and even though I am tired
and even though I don't want to fight anymore
and even though I don't always know what I'm even fighting for I
swing with everything I have

for my father
for my mother
for everyone that did not make it out of Nicaragua when we did
for my sister
for my niece
for my nephew
for every person that I love
for every person that loves me
for every little brown girl that needs to see me survive this round
for every brown body that is no longer with us
for every brown body that was never given the choice to fight

I swing

      and I swing

            and I swing

Theaters in the Fall

I am on the phone with a friend while scrolling through Instagram.
it is Fall and I have just matched with someone new on a dating app
when I see your picture and suddenly I am in my childhood
bedroom

and it's summer

I am eighteen and my parents are asleep across the house. you are
curled up like a cat
in the Papasan chair next to my bed, one hand covering your mouth
to stifle your teenage girl giggles, the other wrapped in mine. it is
1:00 a.m. and my parents would kill us both if they knew
you climbed the fence every night after they went to bed to crawl in
my window
and fall asleep holding my hand after hours of laughing and talking
and listening to music
and pretending we were just friends, pretending I wasn't watching
your mouth every time you spoke, absorbing every beautiful word
not through my ears but through my eyes, hooked to the Cupid's
bow of your lips

Except now it is Fall and I live alone and I have just broken up with
yet another man with nothing more to offer than audacity and
today I matched with a woman for the first time and all I can think
about is how you asked me to listen to "3 Libras" by A Perfect Circle
because you thought I didn't see you
thought I would disappear if you told me what you tried to hide
between the lyrics of songs

and now it is Fall and I never miss a single photo
not even the ones where you stand beside him smiling the most
beautiful smile I have ever seen
as I think about the nights you spent in my dorm room after I'd
gone away to college
my roommate asleep across from us
you the small spoon I cradled against my chest

because we were just friends, friends that went to the movie theater
that one time when I suddenly felt brave enough to place my hand
firmly on your thigh, our faces inching closer, my hand inching
higher, bewitched at the ways I could make your body dance
beneath my touch until I remembered the god I was raised to fear,
opened my eyes, stood, and walked away

and now it is Fall and I think about the message you sent me years
after because a girl walked into the video-game store where you
cashiered
made you realize that you had been in love with me
you were getting married the next month
you met him in the Navy
he is kind and sweet and honest

and now it is Fall and there is a woman in my messages and she is
not you, and she is not you because of that summer, because of my
father, because of god, because I don't know why—the only thing I
know is that it is not summer and I am not eighteen—it is Fall and I
am not afraid anymore and if this is another theater I refuse to walk
away or disappear again

Advice (to My College Self)

I.

Don't pierce your belly button. It looks cute right now that you're thin but your first adult job will be teaching first graders. They will be tall enough to reach your waist and like to grab at things.

II.

Do not drink that entire cooler of sangria. You will never feel more sick in your life and moving will feel like trying to run in the middle of an earthquake.

III.

Study! Do not put off your finals to go on that date! The hot guy in entomology class is a moron and you will find out that he has the personality of a sponge at the next frat party!

IV.

Learn to keep a toothbrush and your textbook somewhere else, because your roommate will sexile you. A LOT! If you don't want the memories of her breaking the top bunk with her boyfriend that one time, then for the love of God, run!

V.

It is OK to send yourself carnations on Valentine's Day when you're single. Just don't forget that they are from you, because it's OK to love yourself. You don't need someone else for that.

VI.

Double major! It is perfectly rational to study both poetry and biology. Own your intelligence

and tell your advisor to shove it because the only one that knows what
you're capable of accomplishing is you.

VII.
That frat boy will rape you, and it will be OK because seven years later
you'll be able to tell the desperate girl on the crisis text line whose
boyfriend just raped her that this is not the end. As she stands on the
edge of her dormitory roof you'll be able to say I have been where you
are—
This is only the beginning. Trust me, I have survived to make poetry
out of my scars.

VIII.
You are not made from the rocks people throw at you. You are only
strengthened by them
because you survived and can walk with your head held high.

IX.
When they call you a spick tell them that your Costa Rican heritage
finds it beneath itself to answer to bigots simply because they cannot
handle
the merengue in your step. The way your hips whip to the salsa heartbeat
that is still going strong. They are frightened by the smell of the sea
in your hair, the tropical sun in your eyes.
It's not their fault that they are foreign
to your kind of beautiful.

X.
Your parents will be disappointed.
But you will still be amazing. You don't have to sandcastle yourself
into their dreams because no one can love sand.

Life will continue its ebb and flow so be the rock beneath your own
dreams
and build your empire as you see fit.
Every castle deserves a queen and you, my love, are royalty.

Return to Las Piedrecitas

The stone statues of Las Piedrecitas
had set their unwavering gazes
towards the borders
towards the future

I have returned to this fountain
at the center of our park
in my mind
millions of times
but today
as my hands stroke
the sun-baked stone
I ask myself
what I am searching for
in this heat

I have tried to find you
in these rocks
hoping to resurrect the bond
we once shared
from these waters
but just as
you are the stoic statues
to me
impossible to crack
and unwavering
in your direction
I am Nicaragua
burning to the ground
and under foreign rule

You have learned to watch the things you love
crumble to ruins
learned to interpret the rising smoke
from the wreckage
while I have spent a lifetime
learning to analyze
the emotion
in stone gazes
and making pillows
out of rocks

Tamales

Standing by the open flame
that is far too hot
a banana leaf gently held
within both hands
I hold it steady over the fire
until it emerges
malleable
"Así lo quieres, o más suave?"
I ask as the leaf burns.
My mother tries
to roll it up
but it is still too hard
Finally it softens up
and is sent off
to be cleaned
This year it is tamales for Christmas dinner
She is teaching us
the art
of long
hard work
and as I watch
a new leaf bend
I know I've found
my own open flame.
I'm at ease here,
with her.

Sanctuary

His body is displayed at the center of the room. My paternal grandfather, eyes closed,
dressed in his best suit. Friends, family, and church members sit solemnly around the
corpse. Here lies the reality of death. Cold, not embalmed, unpreserved—a reality
you can smell.

Death can be hard to sit with.

And I am reminded of my maternal grandmother, her carefully made-up face
greeting the ever-moving line of passing well-wishers.

Here, in this setting, it is temporary, contained to a mere viewing. Sterile.

But not in our lands. My grandfather's body was carefully dressed and moved
to the living room. My grandparents' home fills with guests, guardians that will remain
by his side until morning. My grandfather is the only one sleeping tonight.
Here, his friends take turns sitting next to his body. Some stay pressed to my father
as if trying to absorb his grief.

I remember my mother seated next to her mother's pink wicker casket smiling with empty eyes as the never-ending line of

spectators shook her hand playing their carefully
orchestrated part and peering into the coffin, shaking their heads on
cue.
My mother, the dutiful slave of tradition.

My father begins to cry and the guests shift towards him. They mourn
as one.
In the darkness it is easy to sense each synchronized heartbeat.
And as the morning breaks they stand as one. A few of the men lift my
grandfather
and they begin the walk to his final resting place. My father leads the
way
shovel in hand. A dutiful participant of tradition.

Today he opens the Nicaraguan dirt to make way for his father to rest
deep within the land he loved. Today the earth will take.

My mother does not dig the hole for her mother, her final tears falling
on pink wicker.
My grandmother will never again touch her beloved California soil.

My parents ask each other how they want to rest when their nightfall
comes
My father already knows the exact specifications of his casket and has
his suit chosen
My mother turns to me and says return me to my people's land
Let me be the soil where the flowers take root
Let my spirit echo in the raindrops of the jungle
Let me rest beneath the trees where the macaws sing
Let my final gift be to my land and find peace in the depths of her
rainforest.

Instead of coming to visit a stone come lie down beneath the
blossoming vines and feel my soul and my love all around
Whenever you are sad or hurt or scared and need advice let me be
your paradise
Death is something we all face but instead of just a resting place
I choose to become a sanctuary
A reminder that a piece of me will always remain.

So when you've lost your way listen to the wind that makes the palm
trees sway
and know I'm listening always.

Holy

He showers with a washcloth as my eyes worship
every bend of his Black frame
soft skin smooth beneath the water
His eyes catch my open mouth stare
and he smiles
that sideways
wolf smile
the one that flashes
half of the brilliantly white teeth
behind those lips

I adore

Match erupts into flames
in the pit of my belly
Heat rises up my neck,
brain a fuzzy peach
words dissolving on my tongue
this communion bread evaporating to the heavens

His name sits in my mouth heavy
and sweet like the ripest fruit—
delicious,
mine,
sacred

The warmth of his arms,
this soft place against his chest
is Promised Land

to this wandering heart
tired soul resting beneath his chin
After years spent wasting away,
his lips water to this thirsty mouth

He teaches me new hymns
in the evening
These songs have no words
We practice pitches,
rhythm,
music

This is heaven.

When he holds me close choirs sing,
the congregation of butterflies
in the loft of my stomach rises to greet him
The sacred places
where his feet rest—
holy ground—

I adore

His tattoos scripture
gospels I study with eager fingertips—
tracing them,
committing them to memory
my skin attuned to the valleys
he has passed through

He rinses the lather from his back
and offers me his holy
My mouth forgets the taste of words

this sermon a whimper
this sermon a hum
this sermon a sigh

Tonight we preach—
Thou shalt explore the land and have
dominion over it

His name the prayer
I whisper
when the service ends.

Sugar

My tea set was covered in pale,
pink roses beautiful and delicate.
My table was set and the sun seeped in the window

falling on the stuffed animals. The macaws
outside were singing. Today I wore pink
tennis shoes, hair wildly fell in my eyes.

He asks if he can join the party.
I smile, nod yes. Picking up the sugar bowl
He asks if I know where the sugar is. I frown
in confusion and he tells me he can show me.

It will be years before I understand
consent and its meaning.

I spent so many years after
drinking my tea
unsweetened.

The day I heard he died
I wandered past the storefronts
of the local mall and stopped
in front of a window where a pink tea set
was displayed with tiny flowers
decorating the teapot.

I drove it to the Goodwill store
knowing a little girl would enjoy

this simple luxury
but as I approached the donation window
I stopped
looking down at the box thinking.

Opening it, I removed the sugar bowl
and threw it in the trash. I apologize
to the donation man about the set being incomplete
but he says someone will love it
just the same.

Ordering a sweet tea at the coffee shop next door
I smile, stirring in a packet of sugar,
remembering that beautiful teapot covered in roses.
Yes, someone will love it. Just the same.

Ash

The tears do not come
when the veterinarian asks if we're ready,
syringe in hand,
not when my elderly tabby fixes me
with one final, tired, green-eyed stare
placing his paw
gently in the palm of my hand
as he has done for the past decade
every time I'm sad
as if to reassure

He is more prepared to rest
than I am to let go—

They do not come when he breathes his last
when the steady rise and fall of his body ceases
Manic Monday plays in the lobby
and somewhere another vet announces
a kitten is three pounds today
as our vet nods to me
declaring his transition complete

The tears come when she asks about his body
I am unprepared to consider
what is left behind
when we cease to be

I tell her I will take his cremated remains
his final resting place a reminder
not to wait,
not to hesitate,
not to put off anything or anyone ever again

a reminder that everything we love
will one day turn to ash
there's not a second to waste

Manos

When I look down at my hands,
my hands look just like his;
resting on my new guitar
my hands look just like his.

Tal vez aprenderé un canto hoy
de los que él me cantó
tal vez cuando lo cante yo
más cerca a casa yo estoy

We share these hands, and memories,
we've shared our pain and joy.
Tal vez con mi guitarra
cantaré su canto hoy

Estrangement in Three Steps

I.

The father does not approve of the youngest daughter's engagement
granted the groom is locked in the pen serving his fourth sentence
but she is fiercely convinced he is trying his best
The father calls him trash thinks him animal and the lesser of two
    daughters
suddenly has value compared to her fiancé's insignificance
The girl marries anyway in a dingy chapel
behind his unit—the warden observes
and the groom is allowed to be without handcuffs
at least for the ceremony. There is no cake, no pictures, no family
except for the groom's mother and somewhere a father's heart
feels the "I do" and shatters

II.

The father never asks about his new son pretends to not know how
    to add
does not speak the name for fear of giving it permanence
asks only about her so she stops calling, tired
of the empty chair in every conversation that everyone refuses to
    talk about
tired of hearing the echoes of ghosts that point to a home
she no longer belongs to a past she has forgotten how to miss
The girl gets her husband's signature tattooed on her forearm
the only way to keep him with her and she feels so alone
that the pressure of the needle becomes caress
hoping his name will become home
The father tells her he wants to cut the tattoo out of her skin calls it
    ugly

The girl fights back only to hear him say she is no longer his daughter
What is a Latina girl with no family?
He answers—
and says "nothing"

III.

The girl loses her husband to the deep waters of a drug addiction
three years of abuse and hardship later when she is finally brave
    enough
to file the paperwork she calls the father
but she will still end up navigating the aftermath on her own
The daughter stops going home for Christmas
she does not understand the meaning of family
the word a mere dustpan a tool to shake broken, unwanted things
into the trash can with
The girl goes to Christmas with her new lover's family
watches them laugh, watches him smile with his father,
misses her own finds herself wanting to call
but does not pick up the phone too tired for séances
too weary to try and conjure up his ghost
too depleted to resurrect someone that cares
maybe he never did the girl plans the cover up
for her forearm—a teal typewriter
surrounded by forget-me-nots and roses,
a tribute to three people she loved
that now look out for her from heaven,
her ex-husband's signature will soon
be laid to rest with her father's words
beneath reminders
of people who actually loved her
a burial of sorts
a letting go—
finally aware there is no home
in anyone
that she is the only home she will ever have.

An Ode to Brown Fathers

This morning I woke to sunlight
stretching across my brown skin
stretched these dark arms
and looked out
at the most beautiful green grass

I remembered you.

It's Father's Day
and all I can think about
is your screaming children
I pray
in the only way I know how
with poetry

Today I listened to Nino Bravo's
smooth voice belt out
América, América
the song that reminds me
of my own brown father
and how he left everything
he ever knew or loved
to bring two children
to this land of opportunity
and promise
I don't think I'd use
those words anymore

Children are not the only things
this land is skilled
at tearing away
Nino Bravo sings that when God
thought of Eden
He thought of America
God must have
one hell
of a sense of humor

I would wish you
brown faced migrant worker
a happy Father's Day
but how can I use the word
happy
to describe this day for you
missing your children
in a strange land
without your wife
to soften the blow
I know how fiercely
brown fathers love
I know how fiercely
brown fathers protect

No.

I won't insult you
with happy
instead
I'll wish you
a strong Father's Day

I will hope for strength
I will wish you a day
where you hold your head up
on a spine made of titanium
a day
where you will not let anyone
bow your head

Dear brown fathers
you are at least
on my mind
May you use the strength
your arms have built
building this land,
tilling its soil,
cleaning its lowliest places,
holding the world together
for your little family
to walk tall today
always

Rust

This is how it begins—a slow decay, rust—
traditions dusty and unused, a film of cultural rust

I break my spine to display humility as woman
should. He says "duty." I see rust.

To cover and conceal. To cause damage. To break.
My pride abandoned and grown over with rust

He said beauty is in the ability to bow your head.
My mother learned to make herself small, dress in rust.

My back is iron rod. I cannot bend.
It will not fold into this mold, won't yield to rust

and I am too loud, too quick to raise my voice,
my questions, grenades blowing apart his pride, rust

Bowed heads mean surrender and I do not make habits
of gifting him wars, abandoning my pride to rust.

My stubbornness will be my end but I dig in
my heels anyways, his anger will fade. Rust.

His disappointment will ebb like the ocean back home.
I am battleship. I will break before I rust.

As water always meets the shore, salt to sand
I, Noelia, will find my path. I will not yield or rust.

Roots

Somewhere
beneath this sun
brown hands work the soil
preparing the earth for seeds
wrinkled brown fingers
pull a towel
across a sun-beaten
almost black forehead
as old eyes
look across the dusty fields

Farmer
migrant worker

beautiful
necessary
hard-working soul

Sitting here
on my color-coordinated balcony
surrounded
by Spanish-tile mosaic tables
I think of you
beneath the Central American sun
as I write
this poem
facing the gently flapping
American flag

We have the same sea salt
in our veins
the rhythm of the ocean waves
beats alongside our hearts
our breathing
syncopated to the same
Spanish guitar lullaby
in our souls

We are one

I have worked so hard
to uproot
while you have worked
just as hard
to plant

I think of you
our shared history
and stop digging
hoping there's still seed left
in the surviving soil
hoping it will take root
and blossom
overflowing
until it becomes a forest
reminding me
that even the mightiest trees
need roots

When my white female colleague calls me angry

...during a DEIA+ work meeting on Zoom...

all I can think about is the plane ride—my hand grasping the hand of my father
as the plane soars above the clouds
I am seven and wearing a bow in my hair
the kind that's big and colorful, the kind you can't miss
the one my mother carefully wove into my braid
Under his breath my father hums Nino Bravo's song América
the one which translated says that when God thought of Eden he thought of America

I think about my mother   those early days   trying to teach my father English
trying to explain to him all the rules that don't make sense
how his tongue sounded heavy against the politeness of the language
he tried so hard to cradle in his mouth
I remember how elementary school was the last time my throat ever held my accent
how people at church would tease him because his three sounded like tree
maybe that's why all I notice is how whiteness barks

I think about that day we went back to visit Nicaragua, how I caught a glimpse of myself in the mirror inside a shoe vendor's tent as we walked through the open-air market, the day I was wearing that skirt, and the bright red off-the-shoulder blouse with the flower embroidery and the zipper up the back, my curly hair braided down

one shoulder—how I started to cry because while I looked like a
local in the mirror I had never felt like more of a stranger to my own
reflection and I couldn't remember the last time I'd lied to a mirror

I think about my mother's recipes, the ones she tried to teach me
during the years when all I cared about was fitting into whiteness,
how I never learned a single one, how I envy the Latina girls that
know our dances, how I envy the Latinos with their own inside
jokes they tell themselves in Spanish, only because I never knew it
was OK to rebel, because I never knew it was OK to cling to the
remnants of my culture, how I haven't been back home in over ten
years
how I have a degree in English and still have cashiers at Walmart
ask me questions slowly and loudly

I think about the ways I have made my brown body small
how whiteness requires you to fold to the point of breaking
and then faults you for the shattered pieces
how the last white boy told me every day that I was intimidating
how I learned to fold softness into my words, to look at the ground
when I spoke
to hold my arms close to my body, to breathe before opening my
mouth

how there are few people in this world I have ever felt safe enough to
be angry with
how my anger requires a level of trust,
a level of security clearance that most people are not given,
how my anger is a privilege most people will never have,
how I actually cry when I'm angry,
how the volume of my voice they are hearing during this work
meeting
is my attempt to drown out the terror of being too brown clawing at
my throat

how I wonder if there will ever be a place soft enough for me to just
exist

how I wonder where that girl in the mirror is now
if I lost her for good
if it's too late to call her back
if she's still wearing those bright colors
if she still braids her hair
if her three sounds like tree
if she's keeping our accents safe

A Kyrie for Dreams

A Call-and-Response Poem by Noelia Cerna & Alna

Rocked by the tropical breeze,
lying in your bed,
with Spanish translations of American reruns
rolling through your bedroom,

> reruns that sadly enough
> are too obscene
> for your children to watch
> in English

or Spanish
you dream of a golden land
The Seven Cities of Cibola
translated into Modern Day
and Modern Speech...
English to be sure

> The ever supreme language...

The scent of night jasmine
rocks you to sleep,
and you dream of a land...
The Land.
Everything good is tied up
in that land;
salaries, music lessons, sports,
and peanut butter,
oh, and American Cheese slices

> everything but the values
> you teach your children
> and the language
> you now think is beautiful

You sigh and save,
you scrimp and dream

the value of frugality
you will forget

until, finally,
you cross the sky
and walk into your dream.

Shiny-haired, rosy-cheeked children
grow up in The Land
They can swim, and play flawless basketball.

They can make fun of your children
for speaking
with an accent too

They are part of the choir
and the band
they own T-shirts that proclaim
that they are honors this,
and honors that,

Those honors don't mean
"honorable"

and suddenly, your children,
the focus of your tropical dreams,
lose their heritage,
their pride in the race,
their ties to the past.

A past that no longer
can be seen
as "Modern"

they become mute to their Mother tongue.
They scorn parents, home, and habits.

Since these things
are only the most popular
"trends"

They are ashamed of you,
of their past.

Because years of being teased
have taught them
to be ashamed
of themselves

Their alienation becomes complete
when they no longer wish to,
or are capable of
communication
with those left behind.

Too far away
for anyone to reach

Ties are broken.
The next generation
is twice as distant,
slowly transforming
into a group
melted against the sides
of the great American melting pot.

A pot that threatens
to burn whatever
is left

Becoming part of a homogenous mass,
losing forever the night breezes,
the scent of jasmine...

The things you once
relaxed,
and paid attention to
before you realized
in the new world
there is no time
to think

Cultural orphans
with developmental barriers

because they cannot hear, or see,
or speak.

Without a map
or a sign
telling them
where home now is

And you, on your knees
lift up a Hail Mary,
realizing that your dream
has landed your child
into the cultural circle of Hell,

although it never was
your fault

while, back in your land,
the night breezes gently move
a lace curtain,

Breezes (like prayers)
can move anything
just like curtains
they might budge

where another unenlightened soul
lies dreaming
about the day when
she can leave.

And the lost, younger souls
dream of the day they can return
and remember what they came here for

Love Letter to the Immigrant

Yes, you.

The one holding fragments of an evaporating language beneath
your tongue, crossing oceans so your children can break barriers
instead of soil

To the mother tucking pieces of her native tongue into her
children's backpacks
To the father trading master's degrees for chicken plants
To the children entering classrooms in a country that does not like
natural hair or curls

They will call you ugly, try to wrap your identity within a slur, build
cages around you, call you illegal, make fun of your accent and skin
color

Remember when they try to break you
how your ancestors carried the same skin tone
how you are still beautiful

Do not let them steal the language from your throat

They will try to convince you that tongues cannot carry two
languages,

But remember your accents are landmarks,
reminders of the homes left behind,

Remember every piece of identity you keep is a connection to home
and to those that came before.

Remember that seeds do not concern themselves
with how deeply they've been planted
they just take root
and bloom.

The one in which I work for a church

…of rich, white folks during a pandemic and during the dystopian
   bullshit that is 2020 and wonder while I update their prayer list
   what mine would look like if God and I were still cool…

I would tell God that maybe He shouldn't have said that one thing
about not giving us
more than we can handle 'cause I can't handle any more of this shit
and He and I both know it.
I would tell Him about the white woman in the congregation
who didn't apologize when I corrected the way she had been
spelling my name wrong
for ten months, despite it being in every conceivable location and
spelled correctly.
I would talk to him about the audacity of white women
on full display when she did not acknowledge the correction or
apologize
and then sent the next half-dozen emails to me without using my
name at all
as if I had somehow written myself out of existence by daring to
correct her.
I would tell Him about the way my white boss loves to talk about the
mission trips to Honduras
because what white Christian doesn't love using poor brown kids
like Instagram filters.
I would tell God about the way my white boss only cares about poor
brown kids
when he can use them to brighten up his image
while ostracizing me for speaking out against racism in the
workplace
because once you speak up you are no longer useful as a photo prop

instead you become angry and problematic and they can't have a
filter that talks back
a filter that won't cover their blemishes, that won't cover the years
of inherent privilege that they refuse to acknowledge.

I would ask Him to take me back to the time before July of 1994,
before the plane, and the immigration paperwork, and the day in
the room
where I raised my seven-year-old hand to be sworn in
to a country I didn't realize hated me for the color of my skin
or because of the Spanish in my mouth, back to a time when I didn't
know I was a brown girl.
I would ask to go back to a time when I was playing with my toy
farm animals,
painstakingly lining them up, one right after the other.

I would ask Him to send me back to the time when my neighbors
would show up to our home, with queso frito and pitaya,
where we'd play culebra with the neighborhood kids.
A time when speaking Spanish did not feel like painting a target on
my own back.
A time when being brown was something everyone else was.

I would ask God to take me back to a time when all I was worried
about
was if the vendor with the nieve would be back today,
or if the store on the corner would have that American cereal that I
liked
because my parents had the money to afford it today
because even when they couldn't afford American cereal at least I
could go back to my farm animals,
at least then we knew we were being hunted, at least then the
hunters knew what they were.

It is the hunters that cannot admit what they are to themselves that
are the deadliest.

But I don't pray these days.
I have no need for this country's white Jesus and the brown one I
grew up learning about
hasn't been seen 'round these parts for some time
so I update the prayer request asking for safe travels on a cruise,
and the one asking for blessings on a daughter's move to her Ivy
League college,
attach the updated prayer list to the email and sign my name
knowing it will still be misspelled and no one will care that my name
matters
because why should a brown girl's name matter anyways
when they have enough pictures of them surrounded by smiling
brown kids
to ignore the colonizer's eye staring back at them in the mirror.

Most Holy

When I was like a child
you were the keeper of my Most Holy place,
entrusted with my innermost room.
Your feet
leaving footprints in the undisturbed dust
from the years of unwalked corridors.
You were sacred,
unblemished.
I believed your words to be gospels,
holy.
Your plight my mission field.
You—my sanctuary,
the space I would whisper prayers
knowing they were heard.
Believing you
to be the answer to them all.

I talked like a child.
Offered words like incense
to your attentive ears.
Spoke as if you were savior,
protector,
keeper of promises.
I promised to walk with you
through fire,
to offer my sacrifices
when required.
I swore to worship you forever,
to make you king of my heart.

I thought like a child.
Thought your skilled hands
built these steeples,
remodeled interiors,
laid tiles
mended the very foundations.
Thought the hem of your robes
was what cleaned the dust
from the floors.
Thought you saved me.
I stopped believing in religion
and fairytales
but you made me think gods and men alike
could achieve perfection.

I reasoned like a child.
Believed your anger to be righteous.
Believed I was the broken one.
Believed the confident tone of your voice
when examining my shortcomings
meant you were correct.
Believed the red flags to be tests
of how wholly I could love.
Believing for every piece of myself lost
you would restore it sevenfold.
Convinced myself I was incapable of loving.
Knew deep within me
my sacrifice was unworthy of your altar.

But when I was grown
I noticed the steeple, so beautiful,
that ascended towards god
averted eyes away from the weeds

breaking through the tiles.
Began to see the interior remodeling
was to cover up the way your shortcomings
gutted the original splendor
of the inner rooms.
Realized the newly laid tiles on the floor
sounded hollow beneath my feet,
placed above the vast emptiness
in each promise you whispered
in my temples.
That the foundations beneath my feet
were built on lies
wrapped in pretty smiles
pearly white teeth hiding
the poison in each word you hissed.
A snake in god's clothing.

When I was grown I realized it was my tears,
and constant anxious pacing that kept
the floors clean of dust.
That these sanctuaries were held together
by my strength.
My determination to preserve
whatever pieces of me remained.
Realized I did not need your intercession
because I was the sacred one.
The innermost room mine.
You were an empty ark
pretending to hold holy relics,
taking up space
that could be used for my own blossoms.
So I cleared the room.
Took the ark beyond the outermost courtyard.

Removed every single stick of incense
you taught me to pray with.
I taught myself to pray alone,
removed every lie from my mind,
folded your robes.
I put away childish things.

Janitor

It was my second day on the job at Walmart corporate, by far the most prestigious position
this brown girl had ever been in, and the pressure of the production floor, of the perfectly polished people who might see the weakness hiding behind my trembling bottom lip, forced me to the far stall of the restroom to pull myself together somewhere safe from their vindictive gaze.
That's where I met Maria.

Walking out of the stall, still tearful and shaking, I spotted her kneeling beside the sink.
Her wrinkled hands were wringing out the mophead, the white suds running down her brown fingers.
She smiled warmly and said "hola." I took a deep breath and responded in my mother tongue
trying bravely to smile back. I stared into the mirror smoothed out the silk blouse bought specifically for this job then heard her say "tus padres deben de estar muy orgullosos" and for a moment her words were the salty Alajuela breeze I used to breathe in back home. I smiled and thanked her.
My parents ARE proud of this job.
I began planning my bathroom breaks for ten and three every day when I knew I would find her there.
She'd ask me if the computers were still being pendejos and I would ask if her daughter
had sent her rude Biology professor pa'l carajo and we'd struggle to stay straight-faced
as the tight-laced white folks passed by, nodding their greetings to me while turning their faces away
to ignore Maria.

It wasn't until my third week that I noticed it wasn't just the gringos
whose eyes would roll at her
but the Latinas too. Their expensive heels clicking on the freshly
mopped tile, eyes locked on the mirror
so they could ignore their parents' reflection in her aging, hunched
frame—a reminder of what we might have been. And she keeps her
eyes fixed to the floor on the filth their soles leave behind.
The day one of the Latinas threw a wadded paper towel down and
said "that's what janitors are for"
I asked Maria where home is? She tells me she moved here four years
ago from Guadalajara
hoping to start a bakery making pink and yellow frosted Mexican
bread but the bank
is a border wall
of words and paperwork that she doesn't have the language to scale so
she silently kneels and cleans the fading tile. Maria knows her place.
She reminds me of my father, how his master's degree
became worthless the day he stepped foot on this American dream
soil. His education wasted
as he waded in the blood on a chicken plant killing floor. And I
remember how I promised myself I would never stain my hands
cleaning floors so others could build their success on my back. So I
used my American college education to bleach the Costa Rica out.
Sterilized my island soiled accent for that interview at an ideal job.
Steamed the North Pacific waves of my hair flat for that "exceeds
expectations" review. Now, I think about how brown bodies like
Maria's are the steps I have climbed to become a disaster tourist in
this bathroom that she will never be able to leave.

Maria is throwing trash bags into her cart when she sees me leaving
surrounded by my coworkers.
Her eyes meet mine and I hesitate for a split second knowing if I nod,
or smile or speak in her direction

the brown of my skin will show through the whitewash and the culture I've tried so hard to dress up, press down and clean out will come tumbling through. Maria remains silent and unsmiling waiting for acknowledgement, for permission to speak—

but I walk past her looking down at my hands suddenly feeling dirtier than the tiles
I will never have to clean.

Taco Tuesday

...has been canceled, *motherfuckers.*
We the brown people
are fed the fuck up
So we are no longer feeding y'all
Effective immediately
we are packing up
the burritos, enchiladas, chips and salsa,
fajitas, pico de gallo, guacamole,
tortillas, chimichangas, arroz con frijoles,
tamales, empanadas, hot sauce,
jalapeños

Tres leches just became no leches
for you assholes
We'll take the cute-ass Mexican sweet bread
with the pink AND the yellow powdered topping
and the Cubans?
The Cubans are coming too
the people AND the sandwiches
So there go your platanos,
ropa vieja
and forget about Brazilian steakhouses
We are closing the Mexican food restaurants,
the taco stands,
and taking all the little old ladies
making authentic pupusas with us
We're taking the horchata and
the huevos rancheros,
Yup!

And if losing all of that ain't enough—
well we're taking the Corona and Dos Equis too
because Spanish
Hell, we'll take the mojitos,
we'll take the margaritas cause
that's my cousin's name
Y'all can keep the mariachis though…
Please and thank you.
But we're taking Beyoncé!
Because she was fire on Mi Gente
which means we'll have to take Jay-Z too
We're taking Despacito
however not Justin Bieber
because reasons…
We're taking
Dónde está la biblioteca
cause that's all you motherfuckers
could ever learn to say
We'll also be taking "hasta la vista"

And while you mourn
our food and beer
all those fun things
to try on
and proclaim to love
because they're just soooooo authentic—
we'll take the janitors,
construction workers,
field workers,
plant workers,
washers, seamstresses,
maids, and anyone else
you have seen as nothing more

than a back
to set your foundations on
because it's fun to experience
the things we bring
while spitting on the hands
that brought them.

We will not fertilize your crops
with these beautiful brown bodies anymore!

You'll be left
to rebuild, and clean, and cook, and gather
and do all those tasks
you found to be beneath you alone.
We will take our spices, our flavor,
our rhythm, our music, our histories,
our wisdom, our vibrant lifestyle
and leave you to figure out
your identity
without our culture-
and then we'll take back our children-
because even in the sorrow
of our dangerous and crumbling countries
even in the midst of poverty
and hunger
and murder
they will at least
sleep in our arms
the only place
children should ever sleep

And to anyone who believes
these tiny brown babies

deserve to be caged
like animals—
since we couldn't learn
English good enough for you
We say
Que se valla joder gran hijo de puta
and if you didn't understand that
we say
make your own damn burritos bitches

Brown

It happens when she enters the van. Typical soccer mom van.
Suburban staple.
Her white boss is driving, while she and three white coworkers
discuss the day.

As the conversation ebbs and flows she sits, looking out the window,
watching
the city roll by, suddenly aware she is the only brown girl in this
space.
It is not a feeling of fear that fills her chest but one of sadness.
Suddenly longing to look back and catch a flash of brown
or Black skin amongst the sea of white. She walks past the storefronts
trailing her party,
an island
locked in the Central US.

The door to the restaurant opens and the beat of the Latino music
wafts out with the smells of meat and onions, Spanish words
surround her and she steps into this home. The cooks are all brown.
They turn the carne on the fire as they dance to the music and laugh.
It is loud and warm and smells like a fritanga.
Bright banners hang in rows spreading across the ceiling
the colors warm and inviting. They remind her of the open-air
markets
where the brightly colored shirts hang throughout tents
and the smell of cooking meat wafts between the aisles
as the street vendors call out to the passersby to enter their stores
calling them queens, sweethearts, loves, princesses, corazon.

Wicker lanterns are spaced across the ceiling mingling with the banners
they sway with the breeze casting shadows below
twinkling in the dark room like a mother's prayers in the night
as two parents prepare themselves to bring two little girls to the promised land
hoping they will not forget the histories in their skin.

Laughing with her white coworkers the brown girl bites into her carne asada street tacos
letting the flavor fill her mouth and Narciso Yepes's "Romance"
wafts through her mind reminding her of a time she was a little girl and her father
would serenade her with his Spanish guitar, and her curly hair was beautiful, and her brown skin was beautiful, and she remembers what it feels like to be proud of who she is
so she rides back to the office looking out the window, smiling
and when she reaches her desk pulls the scrunchy out of her hair, fluffs it
into a frizzy mass of curls lets it hang loose around her shoulders
puts her headphones in and ends the day with Narciso
with wild hair, brilliant smile, looking like the little girl her parents raised.

The Text from My Mother Is About Her Upcoming Appointment

contains the words "heart cath"
the rest of the words
a blur
of the non-threatening

I remember the last heart cath
despite her saying not to worry
the way the doctor's mouth
formed around the word "lucky"
rarely do we know
how close we come
to losing the ones we love

But I know:
Three minutes.

I still remember the way
her heart chose revolution
because all of us
be Latina
even our hearts rebellious

My mother
three minutes away from death
how the best cardiologists
were all there that same day
for unrelated reasons

the way that "miracle" sounds different
when you realize
Jesus made water out of wine
only once

The Day a Full Moon Remains in the Sky at Dawn and I Don't Take a Picture

For Karen Hayes (1953–2019)

I knew it was her
Recognized that smile
The bold stance
The larger-than-life glow

She does not ask the sun
for permission
to rise
She does not ask the night
for a leave of absence
Simply lets her fullness
bleed into the dawn

Simply is
Simply shines
Simply gifts the daylight her presence
Bold as brass
in the shimmer of the morning sun
Simply twirls her skirt
at the passing cars
Smiling down cheekily

Phenomenal,
and unapologetic.
She takes her throne despite the growing sunlight,
smiling coyly
As the heat of the day begins to rise
her eyes twinkle with remnant starlight

She's got a thing for hot after all
She joyfully exists
in the fullest, naked bloom
for all the world to see.

She knows her reign extends past nightfall
wants us all to see
crowns do not depend on settings
simply on how queens feel

I watch her in awe
as she remains ahead of my path
Never behind
The other cars melt away as her light
accompanies me all the way to work
and beyond
bathes the path ahead in warmth

I reach for my phone wanting to capture
the morning the moon refused to be outshone
But then put it back down,
Still stunned and overwhelmed
Still reeling from recognition
staring up at her
Letting her exist
Letting her just be
Letting myself be in her presence
reminding myself this did happen
whether a picture exists to prove it or not
That things can just exist
That moments can be just that—
Temporary and fleeting but real

I want to speak
Tell her everything
that has happened in her absence but something tells me she already
    knows
Something about the way her light twinkles around her
tells me she played a part
Tells me she's been knocking on heaven's door on my behalf
telling the powers that be
"This poet? This poet is one of mine"

So I remain silent
Simply let myself sit with her

And she smiles at me, nods her approval
Always guiding me onward
And I watch
And listen
Letting her light speak and say
"I'm still here.
Remember?"

Cathedral

The days following my soulmate's death I am like an abandoned
building…

all cathedral and no music
all architectural bone
and no organ
no heat
no spark
no cold
no light
only echoes of echoes where feelings once were

gutted
his absence ringing in the spaces
between every wall
his shape an empty shimmer of air
in every drafty hallway
his voice a mere memory
of an echo heard in a once-furnished room somewhere

a soundwave
I can't quite place

his absence
is everywhere
every peaceful moment
filled with his nothingness
a wrecking ball
leaving these skeletal remains

vacant
only structural
reaching into the night sky
with exposed frame
hoping a single gust of wind
will not be enough to topple it all tonight.

And Sometimes Grief Is an Unopened Bag of Flamin' Hot Cheetos

the one I bought to celebrate what should have been your thirty-sixth birthday
but cannot bring myself to open.

Sometimes grief hides deep in the tremble of my hands every time I reach for it,
lurks within the terror that says the moment the Cheetos are gone
your ghost will disappear as well
because even though I am healing
and even though I feel stronger than ever there are days I wonder
if I am good enough to hold the attention of a ghost
remembering the day I found out you'd cheated
after having walked through hell for you
realizing you can't be a ride or die if you are riding alone
maybe that's why I'm still on this ride even after you've died
still trying to keep you here
still needing to prove I'm worth your time
still trying to become everything I felt you needed me to be.

No one prepares you for the rage that comes with burying your soulmate when you're thirty-four
how every pregnancy announcement,
                engagement,
                    wedding,
                        home purchase,
                            family photo
                                will hit
                                  exposed
                                  nerves.

How everything when you are in your thirties and have friends
involves all of these things.

I have lost count of how many times a single heart can shatter.

No one tells you how to grieve the only person who has ever held
every piece of your heart
only to break every last bit of it
how do you grieve the man you left because you had to save yourself
how do you explain to the ones that watched you run
how you packed what you could in such a hurry that you left your
heart behind
and you're not sure it has all come back yet
even after you watched his body lowered into the ground

maybe the unopened bag of Cheetos in the pantry
and the memories of the way he looked at me,
that voicemail I saved of his laughter
are the only things that make it possible
to bear the fact that he will never laugh again

Maybe remembering someone's light
is the only way we survive the night.

Walking Our PTSD

The puppy is afraid of the trash truck, the way it clangs metal
against metal against the darkness of the early morning.
He is afraid of the electric box, disguised to look like a rock,
the one that marks the halfway point of our walk down our street.
He is afraid of recycling bin lids, disabled dachshunds, and
the friendly dog that wags his tail and barks a greeting from his backyard.
I feel him pull against his leash to cower behind my legs
but never lose my temper. Instead, I kneel down and blow kisses
when he whimpers, hug him when he quivers. I too know what it is like
to be afraid of things no one else can see.
Sometimes trash trucks can look like monsters in the dark,
sometimes fake rocks can hide dangers only I can sense,
sometimes recycling bin lids can be holes in the sidewalk.
I call him sweetheart and kiss his muzzle,
knowing I am afraid of the sound of keys and closing doors,
knowing like him I am afraid of life's normalities,
how I always wonder when someone tells me they are going to the store
how many times it will take before they don't come back anymore.
The puppy is not the only one who spends his days
staring out windows looking for the car
that holds the one he loves to return. My recycling bin lids
are the extended silences of a phone that does not ring,
my fake rocks the temporary goodbyes that feel like forever
and my trash trucks the emptiness of cold sheets on the other side of the
bed
when I wake up alone in the middle of the night. I know what it is like
to hear bombs lurking beneath the singing of birds,
what it is like to hear the helicopters and blaring sirens
despite the peacefulness of a normal Wednesday night.

I kiss the puppy, tug gently on his leash, and tell him he's coming home
with me.
I tell him I love him and that I'm right here. I tell him WE are going home
and a part of me wonders as we continue our walk
if I am reassuring him or myself, that someday, someone will see the fear
and instead of running will tell me WE are going home,
that I am loved, that they see the trauma but are here to swim against
the only stream I've ever known. So we walk. His tail begins to wag,
thumping against my leg. I blink back tears as he gratefully leans against
my leg
and wish for a reassuring love like mine for him.
We pass the fake rock and the puppy walks with his head held high,
a sign that even the deepest fears can be soothed.

Liturgy for the Lost

Last year you pierced your ears.
You grew up a pastor's daughter
in a denomination that taught you
your body belonged to God and to men
before it could ever belong to you,
taught you jewelry was a sin and piercings were abominations—
relegated to something the lost did.

While most of your classmates wore earrings
from the time they were babies here you are,
thirty-four years old and still learning
how to navigate the holes you chose
less than a year ago.

There are times you feel less than,
times when you have to ask for help
getting an earring in,
there are the really beautiful big earrings
you purchased but are still too afraid to wear.
There is beauty in fear
in knowing you are not ready but can choose when you are.

Religion robbed you of choice for so long,
taught you men could say what was acceptable
for your body, do with it what they wished.
Yesterday you cried
because you couldn't get your left earring to cooperate,
had to call your best friend
have her Facetime you through it.

Know this moment is still a choice.
Know that renovations require moments of breaking.

Today you arranged the new earring stand you bought.
Carefully placed the studs,
unwrapped the heavy pairs of earrings
you so carefully curated.
As you look at the happiness on your vanity,
remember the years you would stare at your classmates' ears
longingly
knowing you could rock the earrings
they chose to wear,
the jewelry they didn't have to hide from their moms,
how you dreamed up the outfits you would wear,
if only.
Know this is celebration.
Breathe in the choices you have made for yourself.

You were once told your body was a temple.
This was the reason you were indoctrinated against piercings,
against tattoos, against choice.
Remember when your Bible was written only men
were allowed to be priests
so it is only fitting they believed themselves gods.
Made you believe choice was a desecration
if it be defilement by man then let it be called worship—
if by you, then let it be abomination.

When you are ready to wear the biggest pair of earrings you own,
remember to brush back your hair,
extend your neck as you walk and let them swing.
Let them be pendants.
Let them be flags.

Let them be beatitudes.
Blessed are they that renovate temples.
For they shall rebuild peace.

This is how temples are reclaimed.
How holy ground is restored.
Let the congregation of those
still in captivity say hallelujah as you walk past.
Let them say god has brought them out of captivity.
And she be looking fine in some earrings.
Let the flash of color from your ears show them a taste of holy.
Let the temple be restored to its former glory.
Let the people say—
Amen

Ghoster

When we first met two years ago our chemistry was undeniable
hours spent talking on the phone
text message threads longer than most of my relationships
At night our shadows would paint the walls of your bedroom
in the light from the living room as we made art with our bodies
Yours, the first body I let touch me after divorcing my soulmate

You once told me no one wanted me to win like you did
Maybe it was I that broke your heart
maybe in the shuffle of things we both left unsaid
it slipped from my hands somewhere and shattered
You once asked me why I never slept over
and I never had a good enough answer
so I let the question hang

As it turns out... I have an answer now
Maybe I sensed it then
Maybe my anger is making me bolder than usual
Maybe I have broken just enough times
that the jagged edges have turned out
but after having spent two years
texting me constantly
asking me to come see you
asking me to pull up
telling me you missed me
perhaps something in your tone made me want to believe
maybe I misunderstood something in what you were so clearly saying
maybe I can still find a way to blame myself
Besides who cares who started the hunt so long as the wolf gets fed...

You asked me why I never slept over
It is now 1:00 a.m. on New Year's Eve, 2021
we are both two years older but our bodies somehow slip easily
back into the rhythm of the dance we once knew so well
and I remember your cologne
you send me home covered in it
and for the first time in many, many months I lie in my own bed
smiling at the scent of cologne
and I wait for the phone calls to begin again
and when those don't come
I wait for the text messages
and when those don't come
I wait for my dignity

You asked me why I never slept over
and I'm sorry it's taken me this long to answer
I never slept over
because I knew if I let myself fall asleep beside you
let you wrap your arms around my waist
let you hold me close while I dreamed
it would mean I trusted you and I have made the mistake
of sleeping next to too many men that could not see the treasure
sleeping beside them
that could not see the power they held in their hands when they'd
reach for me
the men I have known have never left me a feast
never been able to feed me
merely leaving my own carcass at my feet
picked clean
to try and salvage a body from

I am unsure how many more people can lie to me before I build an
unscalable wall

I am less angry at you for disappearing and more angry at myself
for letting my own expectations of you hurt me

men will devour you to avoid the secrets hidden in their closets
knowing if they wound you badly enough
it won't matter whether you call their treachery
lies or omission

And while you, ghoster, may choose to remain unhealed and
insignificant
I know that I will heal from this as well
and evolve to the point
that you will no longer be my type
and because you aren't even good enough to become scar tissue
I am about to turn you into nothing more than memory
and some day when you reach back out
telling me that falling out of touch with me was such a shame
I will look at your message in my phone
only to realize that I completely forgot your name

A Poem for the Tree Growing by the Overpass

When I saw you this morning you had bloomed
Green-sheathed arms reaching for the skies
the sun casting delicate orange, white, pink, and blue streaks
intensifying behind the deep green leaves springing from your
outstretched branches

I don't remember you being this green before today
as if you blossomed overnight

Just yesterday your bare bark arms stretched towards heaven
a plea—almost like prayer—and today you stand confident
glowing in the pale morning light

You are stunning, bold, alive,
Almost as if you too are a survivor of unspeakable things
Almost as if you too have walked through valleys
no one ever thought you'd find your way out of
Almost as if blooming is a revolution
Against all who thought your bare bark was all you'd ever be
A reclaiming from all those who reduced you to nothing more than
your winters

And I swear as the light reflects off the dew drops collecting on your
leaves
that I can feel God and that hope settles on this day
So real I can touch it
It is in this simple act of being,
existing, living, blooming

Saying to the whole world with our green-sheathed arms
that we are more than survivors
We are alive and whole and well
Finding power, purpose and hope in simply overcoming
As we both plant our feet
in the soil we have been given

Dear Timid Latina Girl

You, caramel-skinned beauty.
You with the headband of a thousand colors
keeping the wilderness of curls out of your face,
each woven color flashing glimpses of Spanish tile
and painted ox carts
in reds, yellows, and oranges

sitting cross-legged
the brown skin from your exposed shoulder gleaming in the glow of
your laptop
writing this poem,
this love letter to yourself late into the night

Today your hair is wild, untamed, and taking up space
which is to say
you are in your full goddess form

You are still unlearning the fear of being everything you are
still only comfortable enough to be yourself
when you are here,
in the privacy of your home, alone.
Still navigating the imposter syndrome you fight in your own skin,
still grieving the accent your mouth no longer holds,
still trying to be the "right kind" of Latina

You are the only lover you've ever had
that you felt comfortable enough to be yourself with
You are the only person that has ever seen you dance to Celia Cruz,
that has seen the ways you know your body can move,

that has tasted your homemade chilaquiles,
that has seen the way guayaba and queso together become a
religious experience

You are the only person who has heard
the way you can make your guitar sing in Spanish
the chords and the songs your father used to serenade you with
when you were little
before you were old enough to realize the depths of a brown father's
disappointment
you serenade yourself with those songs now

Beautiful brown girl, you hold so much fear within you
it shows through in the way you haltingly navigate your own
Spanish
even here alone where there is no one to make fun of it
even here as you hesitate to speak the Spanish in this poem
the way you protect it,
keep it close to your chest,
cradle it gently in your mouth
for fear it might slip out and embarrass you
for fear your own shadow might let out a giggle
at the way your tongue forgets words
it has not tasted in years

But it is in these moments where you are your most radiant
dancing with your only partner—the broom to Banda Blanca
the way your body slips into a trance
tracing steps your ancestors once swayed in
when you tease your black cat by calling him necio
because no English word fits him better than that
how you call your pets mis amores
how you still call yourself pipita

because it is what they called you in your father's lands
and it is the kindest thing he has ever named you

Someday mija you will heal enough to let your brown skin show
one day you will love yourself so much that you won't care to hide her
until that day comes corazón
you are still brown when no one sees you make queso frito
you are still brown when no one hears you sing Mocedades
you are still brown when no one hears you play Samba Pa Ti

more importantly cariño
you are still brown even when your father decides he only has one
daughter
even now that he has stopped playing his guitar with you
even now that you are not the Latina he hoped for
you are brown and your learned fear does not diminish your magic
you are learning to love your skin in ways you couldn't before
the Pacific Ocean remains an ocean whether called such or not
she remains deep and powerful without need of acknowledgement
she was who she was before she was even named
as are you reina

Until you are ready to step boldly into the world as everything you
are, these quiet celebrations are enough. You are enough, brown
girl... you always have been.

Genesis

The women in my family are all creatives,
my father as well—
but his mind works better with numbers.
Must be why he knows I am only ten percent like him,
bearing hands identical to his,
hands that play guitar like him.
But my hands no longer fold in prayer,
can't seem to leash my identity the way he'd like me to.
I am ninety percent of my mother's kindness
this the only part of her he thinks survived him
A man of god of course desires to tame the earth
and all that is upon it
that is to say my father tried to burn down the wilderness
of my mother's willpower long ago.

I spent my childhood watching him try
to force her into the doormat-shaped role
we Latinas are raised to fill for our men
as only their mothers can be brave or magic
but only enough to raise the men that will then break their
daughters
and so on...

I have long ago stopped paying mind to his ravings
hands and kindness foundations but not the whole of this temple.
Fire be as holy a god...just ask Moses-
fire, what sent him to Egypt
delivered his people from chains
Fire can be the greatest Genesis

My mother is quiet these days
her warrior song hidden behind the night of my father's
expectations
but even silent warriors keep their flame
still flicker even when hidden away
and my mother has clung to enough of her heat
to whisper it to me when he leaves the room
calls me her hawk
calls me her un-cageable thing
calls me wild

The doctors say they are concerned about her heart
unsure of how many more beats it holds
fear is strong enough to freeze even the most powerful of flames
and her days appear to be numbered
I am unwilling to consider if my fire is strong enough
to survive without her tinder
I watch her grow more tired
notice the ways she leans against me when we are together
as if trying to gift me her remaining spark
how she cups my face in her hands
tells me I am a wonder,
tells me to run from any one that does not call me miracle,
tells me I am brave
this her way of saying I cannot buckle
this her way of saying I must hold on
this her way of saying I have a six-year-old niece,
her way of saying I have a one-year-old daughter, two brown girls
we love
speaks with an urgency although we do not say the reason why out
loud

she calls to tell me about her latest doctor's visit
speaks about their concerns as if she is reciting a recipe
pauses and then whispers that I make her brave
the women in my family are all creatives
but I am the only one that has ever openly defied my father
the only one that has ever survived his gospel
but my mother is strong enough to turn herself into burning bush
turn my niece and my daughter into Egypt
turn me into liberator
commands me to break the cycle
commands me to heal the generational wounds
that she was not able to mend

we rarely talk about fire's ability to heal
how soil requires flames for what's new
how it can be healthy
and my mother knows she is old growth
wants her granddaughters to sit beneath the shade of healthier trees
even though she might not live long enough to see it
tells me not to be afraid
makes me promise I will not run from my power
makes me promise I will do what she couldn't
"everything must come to an end" she says
"and I have gifted the world a phoenix"
tells me I was built to survive this heat
that sometimes to heal we must first burn
tells me our girls are lucky to have me
tells me to teach them to be strong
the "when I'm gone" implied
hovering like the flicker of a flame right before it turns into smoke

The caller on the crisis line tells me about her trauma

...and then asks me if I believe it is possible to come back from
something that has completely broken us...

...and I want to tell her about the dozens of times I have crawled
my way out of the abyss
how that first breath of air when your head breaks above the surface
of the water again
feels like God himself is breathing into your lungs
how that singular moment makes you realize what praise feels like
all the times I have held the shattered pieces in my hands
sure that this is how it ends

the kind of pain that makes you wonder
if you will ever be able to breathe right ever again
how I am familiar with pain that leaves you paralyzed
the kind that terrifies you because you wonder if you are dying
Is it possible to drown from a broken heart?

I want to tell her about the days when hiding in bed
was the strongest thing I could do
how I have cried myself through a hundred lonely nights
how I have wrapped my arms around myself so tight
for fear of unraveling into ribbons
how pain has been a boulder resting on my chest
how many times I have been sure this breath
is the last one

I want to tell her about the days I have woken up
only to realize I am still breathing

                              still smiling
                                    still here
                                          stronger than ever before

I want to tell her about the way you laugh
after coming back from something that should have left no survivors
that deep-in-your-belly laugh
that forces you to throw your head back
makes you wonder if perhaps
you have gone a little mad
perhaps the madness is what helped you survive

I want to tell her about the times I have looked in the mirror
and been shocked at the warrior staring back
how many times I have fallen in love
with the oceans behind my eyes

I want to tell her how you will never truly feel like a badass
until you have returned from the dead
with an updated wardrobe,
a new hairstyle
and a new tattoo
as if surviving the apocalypse is just super casual
just something we do on a Friday night
because fuck hot girl summer
coming back from the dead
be the best glow up
it comes with a bonus of giving zero fucks
and an increase in don't need no man,
don't need no job with THAT level of stupidity fearlessness

I want to tell her that this is the origin story of a true goddess
How these are the things that make us rise
to the level of what we are truly worth

But we are not allowed to share personal details on the crisis line
Understandably so
I answer and I say
"Yes. I know it is."
And this is also truth
It is possible.
It is.
It is.
It is.

Acknowledgements

I have millions of people to thank—but I will do my best to name as many as I can in one page. This collection would not exist without the countless professors, writers, mentors and friends that have read every version of these poems and of this collection and offered advice and guidance.

A special thank you to Professor Wayne Zade. This collection was inspired and gently guided into existence by his encouragement and commitment to giving a shy brown college girl room to find her voice. Thank you for being willing to write the foreword for this collection when my big dream of publishing this book finally came true.

Thank you, also, to Dr. David Collins, Dr. Debra Brenegan and Dr. Carolyn Perry—who alongside Professor Zade became my home away from home and encouraged my writing. Thank you for your guidance, for believing in me and for cheering me on all these years later.

Thank you to every organizer and organization that has booked me for readings and workshops and for every single person that has heard me read and held space for my work.

A tiny shout out to Wes Bishop and Professor James Hutchings for being some of my biggest, long term and most constant supporters.

Thank you to J.K. Fowler of Nomadic Press for giving me the yes for this manuscript that I waited ten years for and to Diane Goettel of Black Lawrence Press for taking on this little book.

A big thank you to Max, Brody and Naz for their unwavering friend-ship and support—I am able to celebrate this book as a sober writer and a sober mother because of your love and guidance over the years.

Finally, a big thank you to the following publications for including the following pieces from this collection:

North Meridian Press (2019 issue)
"Brown"
"Rust"
"Tourism and Soda"

NWA Girl Gang Blog
"Brown"

Plants & Poetry Journal (June 2020 issue)
"A Poem for the Tree Growing by the Overpass"
"Roots"

The Revolution (Relaunch) (2019 issue)
"Janitor"

Notes

The bold text in "A Kyrie for Dreams" is a poem written by my mother, Alna.

Photo: Brandon Watts

Noelia Cerna is a Latina poet based in Springdale, AR. She was born in Costa Rica and immigrated to the United States at the age of seven. She received a Bachelor's degree in English from Westminster College in Missouri. Her poems have been published in audio form in *Terse. Journal* and in print in the *The Revolution [Relaunch]*, the *Girl Gang blog*, the *Plants and Poetry Journal* and *The North Meridian Review*. Noelia is a book editor for the *North Meridian Review* and an award-winning writing mentor for Pen America's Prison Writing Mentorship program.